*The Pyrography Begi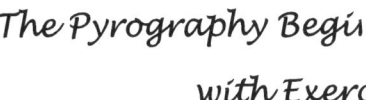*
*with Exerc*

*Learn to Burn with Step-by-Step Instructions with Introduction to Basic Tools, Techniques, Modern Wood Burning Textures and Patterns, and Sample Project Ideas*

By

*Clayton M. Rines*

## Acknowledgments

This book could not have been written without the guidance and generosity of everyone I have come in contact with one way or another. Your influences are all over this book. Thank you.

## Dedication

This book is dedicated to everyone seeking knowledge out there.

**Copyright © 2019 Clayton M. Rines**

The author retains all rights. No part of this document may be reproduced or transmitted in any form or by any means, electronic or mechanical, including photocopying, recording, or by any information storage and retrieval system without permission in writing from the author. The unauthorized reproduction or distribution of this unique work is illegal.

## Disclaimer

All the information contained in this book is purely for educational activities only. The writer does not assert the accuracy or wholesomeness of any info gotten from this book. The views contained within the pages of this material are those of the author in its entirety. The author/writer will not be held accountable or liable for any missing information, omissions or errors, damages, injuries, or any losses that may occur from the use of information gotten from this book.

# *Bonus Book*

Thanks for buying this amazing book. To appreciate your unending support, we are giving you a great book on Pour Painting that will bring to the forth your painter's instinct. You will derive unending hours of pleasure from practicing the beginner techniques you will learn from this book. Look out for invaluable periodic bonuses in your mailbox.

Download the book by clicking or typing the link below;

<https://bit.ly/2LwTK4Q>

Cheers

*Clayton M. Rines*

# Contents

*Introduction* ............ 11

*Knowing your tools* ............ 16

*Guidelines for Beginners and Pros* ............ 19

*Clean Pen Tip* ............ 20

*Colored Pyrography* ............ 20

*Switch off the pen* ............ 22

*Your choice of design* ............ 23

*Picking and preparing the right Wood* ............ 24

*Pyrography Tips and Tricks* ............ 27

*CHAPTER ONE* ............ 36

*The Basics* ............ 36

*The Burning Surface to be worked on* ............ 36

*Tanned Leather* ............ 37

*Wood* ............ 38

*Gourds* ............ 38

*Buying Wood Burning Pens* ............ 39

*Pens with no temperature control* ............ 40

*Rheostat wood-burning pens* ............ 40

*Changing temperature pens* ............ 41

*Changeable Tip Pyrography Pens* ............ 41

*The Solid tip Pyrography Pens* ............ 42

*Copying the Patterns* ............ 42

*Cleaning of the Pen Tips* ...................................... *46*

*Sealers* ............................................................... *49*

*The Wood Patina* ............................................... *51*

*Your Safety* ........................................................ *53*

*CHAPTER TWO* ................................................. *60*

*The Pyrography Machine and You* ................... *60*

*Attaching the Burning Nibs* .............................. *61*

*Practice holding the burning pen* ..................... *62*

*Powering on the Unit* ........................................ *62*

*Temperature Change* ......................................... *63*

*Powering off* ...................................................... *63*

*CHAPTER THREE* ............................................. *65*

*The Pen Tips* ...................................................... *65*

*Writing and Outlining* ...................................... *68*

*Fill Texturing* ..................................................... *68*

*The Scrubbie Shading Technique* ...................... *69*

*Fine Lines Formation* ........................................ *70*

*Texture Patterns* ................................................ *70*

*The Flat Spear Shader* ....................................... *71*

*The Curved-edge Spear Shader* ......................... *72*

*The Wide-wire Square Shader* ........................... *72*

*The Position of your Hand* ................................ *74*

*How to hold a Pyrography Pen* ......................... *76*

*CHAPTER FOUR* .................................................. 79

*Burning Lines* ................................................. 79

*The First Burns* ............................................... 79

*Lines*............................................................ 80

*Direction Alteration*..........................................81

*Change of Speed* ..............................................81

*Play around with different nibs* ............................ 82

*Shading Methods for Beginners*............................. 82

*Shading Light Tones*......................................... 82

*Shading Dark Tones* ......................................... 83

*Progressively Darker Tones* ................................. 83

*CHAPTER FIVE* ................................................. 85

*Your Choice of Wood*......................................... 85

*Burning Words in Wood*...................................... 86

*Getting the Wood Surface Ready*............................ 87

*Transferring Letters to the Surface*........................ 87

*The Image Transfer Pyrography Tip*....................... 88

*Your tools* ..................................................... 89

*Putting the Wood Burner to use* .............................91

*Constant Speed*.................................................91

*Burning the Numbers or Letters* ............................ 92

*Temperature Alteration*..................................... 93

*Darkening the Letters*....................................... 94

*Final Applications* ................................................... *95*
*CHAPTER SIX* ....................................................... *97*
*Exercises* ............................................................. *97*
*Wood Burning Project Ideas* ................................ *97*
*Key Holders* ........................................................ *97*
*Door Decorations* ............................................. *101*
*Fancy Napkin Holders* ....................................... *103*
*Cup Coasters* ..................................................... *105*
*Picture Frame* .................................................... *109*
*Hair Rings* .......................................................... *111*
*Pyro Wall Clock* ................................................ *115*
*Other Book(s) by the Author* .............................. *121*

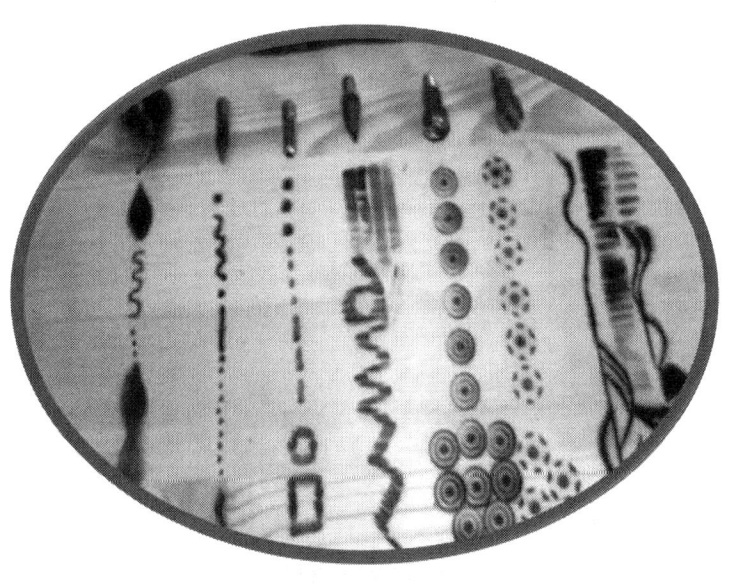

## Introduction

### Pyrography

The term pyrography has its origin in Greek, and it means *pur graphos* (fire writing), and it has been in existence since man discovered fire. Evidence of ancient men practicing this beautiful art can be found on the walls of caves and other structures.

Writings, drawings, and other messages were inscribed and drawn on wood, walls, leathers, gourds, and other surfaces to pass messages, honor gods or to beautify the environment. Going back to the times of the ancient African men, the Egyptians, and in Asia, there are quite a lot of pyrography artifacts which points to the skills and ability shown by craftsman during those times. This art was commonly known as fire needle writing or drawing then. This process gave the artisans and avenue through which they got to showcase their skills and bring the most common objects to life.

With the discovery of fire came the art of pyrography, which employs the use of a heated sharp-pointed object to draw and write. A metal that is heated in fire is mostly used in the drawing of beautiful artworks and other designs. Wood burning is another term used to describe the art of pyrography in putting their skills into practice on a variety of surfaces.

Traditionally, pyrography was a form of art used in designing and decorating musical instruments and a variety of tools and items. Guitars, jewelry boxes, kitchen utensils, hairbrushes were etched with signature art to make the piece unique and to show it belongs to a particular individual. Nowadays, however, the technique has gone a step further in the evolutionary scheme of things by actually burning designs on surfaces that are blank and devoid of any embellishments to convey on such pieces artistic values.

The pyrography pens are a relatively recent invention that has given rise to more elegant pieces of equipment.

The primary tool used in drawing and writing in pyrography is a heated metal tool, but in this age and time, you can make use of a whole array of tips in discovering and giving your piece of work that distinct look to make it unique and stand out. There are pyrography tools that are quite similar to the soldering iron, which allows you to draw solid lines, and there are others that enable you to perfect fine fainted shaded lines. The amount of pressure that you apply to the surface with the drawing tool will also determine the tone that can be obtained.

The types of woods that are used in pyrography are usually light in color, e.g., sycamore, beech, and birch are excellent surfaces for drawing on due to the light grain and color. Your choice of wood will be determined by the outlook you have in mind for your finished work.

It is essential that no matter your choice of wood, it should not be treated, avoid particle boards or pressure-treated boards as such materials have undergone some form of chemical processing or the other. When you apply your pyrography tool to such a piece of wood, the chemicals in the material are set free. If you are not putting on protective gear, you will most likely inhale the toxic fumes.

The fumes are not the only harmful substances that are released when you burn wood, resins, sawdust, and wood shavings can also cause serious health problems if you don't adequately protect yourself.

With your materials ready, safety check put in place; you can begin to pour your skill and fine art onto the piece of wood. Your design can either be transferred to the wood surface by making use of a graphite paper/tracing paper, or you can draw straight to the wood surface with a pencil. Once the image is on the wood surface, the burning can begin. The range of items that you can put your signature design is determined by the limit you put on your imagination.

To get started with wood burning, you will need to get a few basic supplies which include the following;

Wood burning pen

Pyrography machine

The wood sample on which you are going to burn

Sandpaper

The design you want to wood burn

Tape (masking paper)

Carbon paper/tracing paper/graphite paper

## *Knowing your tools*

The wood-burning pen is a relatively easy to use tool for pyrography. It is shaped like your everyday pen, which comes with a metallic tip that heats up when the device is connected to a power source and switched on. Most wood-burning pens have temperature controls, which gives you the ability to lower or increase the temperature of the device depending on the type of art that you are working on at the moment. Taking an in-depth look at the pen, you will notice that it comes with a variety of tips to be used for different aspects of creating a piece of work. They can be used for shading, straight lines, rounded lines, curves, dots, etc. Most wood-burning machines are built in such a way that the pen does not sit directly on the bench; they come with a metal stand to ensure your safety and other implements that might be on the workbench.

To get started, there is a need for you to understand, know, get familiar with the wood-burning pen and other tools that you will be using during the process. For starters, pick up a piece of wood that can be used for practice, connect your wood-burning machine to a source of power, and switch it on and let it heat for a few minutes. You can then proceed to carry out a few test runs on the wood with the set of tips that can be fitted to the pen. After using a tip to draw and you want to change it, switch off the device and let it cool down properly before switching to the next tip, then heat it again before use.

During these practice sessions with you getting to familiarize yourself with the pen and burning on wood, ensure that you don't rush, hold onto your pen firmly and draw deliberately, slow, and steady on the wood. If you are in a hurry, there won't be proper burning that will make the artwork as desirable as it should be. Take your time and be steady as you embrace this new found love.

Here are a few essential tips to be kept close;

When wood-burning and there is more smoke than should be, there is the probability that the temperature of the pen is way too high, and this will impair the quality of the burn in addition to smoke inhalation, which can cause adverse health conditions if you are not adequately protected. To ensure that your burn is smooth and of high quality, turn down the heat of the pen to reduce considerably the amount of smoke generated.

Have a wet towel handy to clean the tip of the wood-burning pen every few minutes. This removes the inevitable wood burn residues that accumulate during the burn process.

Your safety should always be the top priority when wood burning. Your sense of awareness should be top-notch. The tip of the pen is extremely hot when switched on, and it should not be left lying on the table in that state, and it should also not be allowed to come in contact with any other object at any point in time. The pen should be placed in the metal holder when not in use. When changing the tip, even after you have left it for a few minutes to cool down, make use of a pair of pliers in removing the tip and fixing a new one.

## *Guidelines for Beginners and Pros*

As a beginner or a pro, there is a need for you to be aware of some essential guidelines that will help you during your wood-burning sessions. It doesn't matter if you are a pro or a beginner; we all keep learning new and helpful tips every day. Your level of understanding about pyrography is limited to how far you have decided to push the boundaries of your artistic, creative endeavors. Notwithstanding your creative genius or not, there are a few rules that should guide your burning process.

## Clean Pen Tip

It goes without saying that the pen must be cleaned at all times. While you are wood-burning, there is a constant accumulation of carbon at the tip of the pen. This inevitably causes your smooth and light strokes from the burn to be dark and unsightly. Getting black strokes when they are not needed in your work can be quite annoying. Black colored strokes are not ideal in the scheme of things when it comes to wood burning. To avoid this, clean the tip of your pen always.

## Colored Pyrography

When wood-burning, adding some shade of colors to your work makes it more attractive and brings it to life! If you have been wood burning for a while and never added any forms of colors to your work, you have been missing out on a lot. It is not absolute that you add colors to your work, but try to envision how your next artwork would look with a few shades of color here and there. The choice is ultimately yours.

To add some color to your work, make use of either a watercolor crayon or watercolor paint. The watercolor pencil is the best option for beginners who don't have much experience in coloring pyrography arts. On the other hand, however, if you are a pro and comfortable with coloring your works, the watercolor paint or watercolor crayon can be used.

To begin painting your burnt design, put in a few drops of water to the crayon, and use a soft brush to mix and apply it to your work. Always wash the brush thoroughly after the application of each color before changing to another.

Painting your work is not just about making it look unique; it is also about making use of only the very best watercolor crayon or watercolor paints. Do not cut corners when it comes to the quality of coloring materials to be used. Go for the very best in aiming to make your work look as good as possible.

## *Switch off the pen*

Turning off the pen when it is not being used is a slip that a lot of wood-burning beginners and some pros are guilty of. The pen should under no circumstances be left on when you are not making use of it. The pyrography pen is not a tool that should be played around with; it's a serious art tool that can also be quite dangerous and cause bodily harm if mishandled. It may seem simple enough to turn off and then remove the device from the power source, but it is often the most common cause of potential burns and fires. This safety guideline shouldn't be taken for granted.

## Your choice of design

When I started with pyrography, I chose the picture of a small house with the background of rolling hills. You don't necessarily have to go with this design as there is an almost infinite amount of designs that you can choose from. In the beginning, you can work with relatively simple black and white works. As you build up your skill levels, you can introduce more sophisticated approaches in shading and color applications.

You might be a bit confused about which design to work on. You can go online and search for illustrated images in black and white, "wolf black and white illustration," "clouds black and white illustration." " flowers black and white illustration," "skyscraper black and white illustration." The design you choose to burn will be correlated to your skill levels in pyrography. Go with relatively simple designs as you start, designs that have more straight lines, a few curves, and some shadings or no shadings at all.

You have now picked a design, and getting the right size to burn on a piece of wood will be the next step. The size of the design should be able to fit in comfortably into the piece of wood you have available. In case you want a design burnt onto a piece of wood, and you don't have the appropriately sized wood on ground, you might have to reduce the size of the image and if that is not an option, then ordering for the size you want will be the next logical step.

## Picking and preparing the right Wood

There is almost no type of wood that cannot be used in pyrography. When a piece of hardwood is used, it will require a higher temperature for it to burn while a softwood will need a relatively lower temperature. When a piece of wood has been selected and if it slightly uneven or with a lot of bumps, make use of sandpaper in smoothing it well while flowing with the grain of the wood. A quick one here; when burning, try as much as you can to burn along the grain of the wood than going against it.

The project you have in mind will determine the type of plain raw wood, already cut designs, or already pre-fabbed projects you will be working on. If your projects are on already cut designed pieces of wood or pre-fabbed, you will readily get such pieces of wood at any supplies store close to you. It will also save you the troubles of sanding the wood.

## Poplar wood

## Birchwood

Place the design on the wood

Align the piece of paper with the design on the surface of the wood.

Draw the design

Using a dark pencil, draw or trace the image on the piece of paper onto the wood.

Burn

After the image has been transferred from the paper to the wood surface, you can then proceed to burn it. You can also incorporate some elements of shading and coloring into the burnt design as you desire.

## *Pyrography Tips and Tricks*

During the burning process, carbon residues will continue to accumulate on the tip of the pen so much that when you make light strokes with the pen, it will come out dark. Follow the instructions of the manufacturer as to how to clean the tip of the pen.

The color of the burn is determined by how fast and the amount of pressure you apply to the wood with the burning pen. If you are all about a light-colored image, the pen should gently touch the surface of the wood in swift flows. The longer the pen touches the wood with an increase in pressure, the darker the lines will be.

Only copy lines of the image that you need onto the wood in setting the tone for the image. When you burn pencil lines on the wood, it fixes into the project, and getting it out when you are done with the burning will be almost impossible.

With the different types of wood burners out there, temperature control plays a vital role. If your wood burner has temperature control, turn down the temperature to the lowest depending on which part of the design you are working on at the moment. When you burn a part of the design lightly, you can always come back to apply a darker shade onto it. However, once you burn dark lines onto the wood where there are supposed to be light lines, it will be a mission impossible trying to lighten it. If the burner you have doesn't have a temperature setting, start immediately with the burning of parts of the projects that have light lines as the tip of the pen starts to heat. As you continue to use the pen, it will heat up, and you can then progress to the darker areas of the design. If you want to work on the lighter areas again, you will need to turn off the wood burner, unplug it and allow it to cool down for a few minutes before using it again.

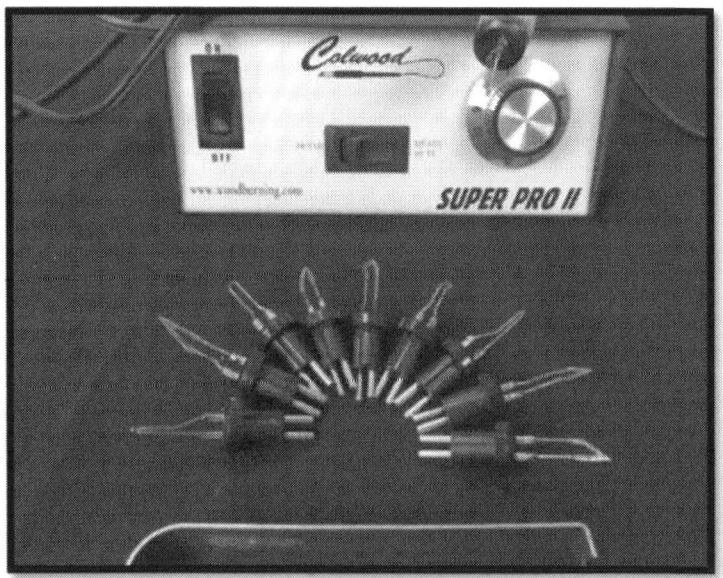

Always start from the lightest part of the project before moving onto the dark parts.

The application of shadows to your project gives it a robust and realistic feel. As you develop your skills in pyrography, include the shading aspects into your works.

Burn along with the flow of the grain of the wood. If you are burning a straight line of an image, the strokes from the pen should be in a straight line with the grain of wood across the board.

When you burn a lot of fine light lines within a space, it will either appear dark or light, depending on how many lines you pack into that space.

The number of outlines you make use of should be as minimal and should only be incorporated into the image if the distinction between certain parts can be problematic.

Practice makes perfect, so before you start on your first project, burn lines of different shades, patterns, tones, etc. on a scrap piece of wood to perfect your art.

The use of textures in a pyrography project helps in making parts of an artwork stand out. So the application of texturing should be incorporated into your works.

With elements of an image that are closer to you, they would appear lighter than those that are much farther away.

For a work that will appeal to you and potential clients, there should be variety in the types of pen tips that you have and make use of. There are brands of pens that allow you to interchange the tips depending on the type of burn you want to carry out. This is something you should have at the back of your mind when buying burning pens as some pens don't have the feature of interchangeable tips.

# I

*Interchangeable tip*

The Writer, Shader, and Skew are the essential tips that you will be making use of in your tool kit. Though there will be other tips in the box, the tips mentioned above will be the busiest.

Shaders come in different forms, and you should pick that which can perform the majority of the shading you want to carry out in any project at any one time. In the bent spear shader, you have a reliable tip that can deliver delicate shades, and more exceptional works in large areas too.

The skews also vary with the round-heeled, and flat skews been the most unique and performing a lot of functions. The round-heeled skew should be your choice here, though, due to its ability to be used in almost any position when compared to the flat skew.

With the writing tips, the ball stylus and the fine tip are versatile and can be used for almost any writing burn that you want to perform.

(A)

(B)

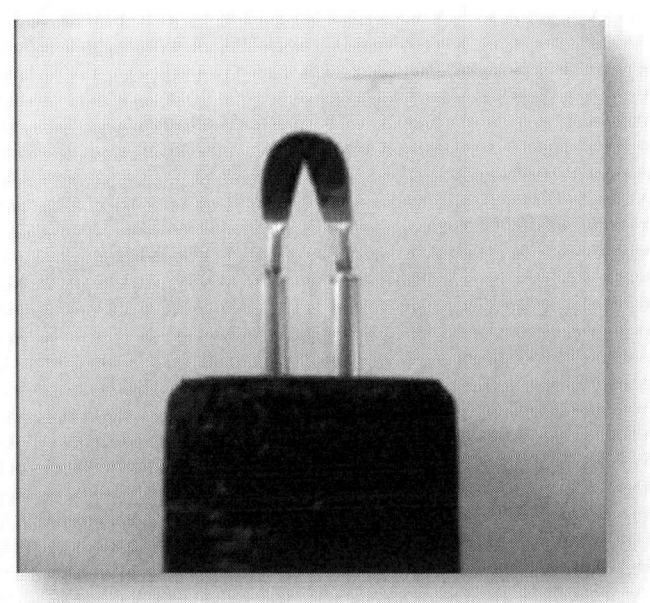

(C)

A - The Skew

B - The Fixed Pen tip

C – The Shader

# CHAPTER ONE

## The Basics

In wood burning, some essential parts are to be considered for a successful operation, and they include the following;

- The surface to be worked on
- The pyrography unit
- The type of tips
- The design you want to recreate on the surface medium
- The pathway to be used in bringing the design to life

Now let's go into details of the different parts.

## The Burning Surface to be worked on

The types of surfaces that can be burned varies, and as long as it is a naturally occurring surface, you are good to go, e.g., gourds, wood, tanned leather, paper mache, paper, etc. You should stay away from any material that has undergone any form of treatment with potentially harmful chemical substances or painted. Such materials will produce noxious and harmful toxic gases when the hot tip of the wood burner comes in contact with the surface.

## *Tanned Leather*

Leather that has been tanned with vegetable extracts is one of the best surfaces to burn on. Leather comes in a variety of forms, which ranges from purses to wallets, book covers to large pieces. With leather, you are given an array of opportunities to work on the media. With the weight variation of leather types, you can pick one as determined by the type of project that you want to work on. Here are the commonly available leather weights; the heavy leather (1/4"), the light leather, which ranges from 1/64" to 1/8". Leather also comes in suede or dyed in different colors; this negates these leather types from been used in pyrography as they have been treated. On the other hand, the suede has an uneven surface that will not give smooth, even lines when burnt.

## *Wood*

The go-to choice of pyrography woods is the poplar and basswood. They are light in tone, have nicely arranged grains, and come in thin sheets that are suitable for burning. Woods that are lightly colored will be a significant determining factor of the projects that you can carry out on them. With the poplar and basswood, you can burn a broad spectrum of color as to when compared to other darker wood shades like the black walnut, which might require more burning on the darker tones.

## *Gourds*

When dried to preserve it properly, gourds are excellent surfaces for burning projects. With the unique composition of the surface, you are offered a distinct proposition for your burning designs. The gourd can be sliced into whatever shape you want it to become; a cup, vase, bowl, or whatever you want it to be. Before you start working on the gourd either during the cutting or burning, put on protective gear.

## Buying Wood Burning Pens

As a beginner or a pro in the beautiful art of wood burning, selecting the right wood-burning pen will serve as the foundation for your works. You must lookout for the type of pen that will align with your kind of art. There are three significant types of pyrography pens;

Rheostat wood-burning pens

Changing temperature pens

No temperature control pens

## Pens with no temperature control

This is a basic wood-burning pen that most beginners are likely to use. The pen has the appearance and heft of a soldering iron, and it is more of an instrument used for a wide variety of functions other than wood burning. For folks who are passionate about the fine art of pyrography, this pen would not be found a mile around you. Due to the weight, length, and girth, your hands would get tired quickly, and your project wouldn't be as elegant and as detailed as you would want.

## Rheostat wood-burning pens

There is a temperature control mechanism installed on this pen. With this feature, you would be able to fashion your desired outlooks onto your works. You would be able to create darker lines and also lighter strokes, which will add more details to your projects. This is a level that other pens cannot attain.

## Changing temperature pens

If you are particularly serious about your craft and are willing to invest in it, then this is the best piece of tool you should include in your work table. The pens are generally lighter and smaller because the temperature control mechanism is not installed directly on the pen itself. Due to this design, you can work for more extended periods without your hands getting tired as when compared with other pens with a more substantial bulk. Based on this design, they are a perfect fit for most hand sizes, from persons with larger hands to those who have small hands.

## Changeable Tip Pyrography Pens

These types of pens give you the leeway to perform a whole lot of tasks with your pen. The pen has the functionality to be fixed with a wide range of tips depending on the project aspect that you are working on at the moment. In addition to the tips that came in the box with the pen, as time goes along and you get more comfortable with your art, you can begin to fabricate your tips. The cost of getting these fantastic tools is easy on your pocket.

## The Solid tip Pyrography Pens

Unlike the changeable tip pens, the solid tip pens cannot be changed, thus meaning that you cannot have varied results to your artworks. Your works can, however, give amazing results when varying solid tipped pens are used. The advantage of the solid tip pen is that the tips are quite strong, with a higher rate of heat delivery to the tip. Since the pens are fixed with individual tips that cannot be changed, you will have to get a few pens to be used for different aspects of your work.

## Copying the Patterns

After you must have gotten the design you want to burn, the next logical step is to copy or transfer the image to the surface. Two significant materials can be employed in this process; the graphite paper and the carbon paper.

To begin with, you place either of the paper types under the paper pattern and put it on the surface where the burn is to be carried out on. You then begin to gently trace the pattern on the paper onto the burning surface. The trace will be transferred onto the wood, leather, or gourd in fine lines onto the work surface. During the transfer process, ensure that you work as carefully as possible because once the transfer is done, it is almost impossible to remove after you must have carried out the burn.

Another method of transferring images onto the burning surface is by making use of a pencil to shade the backside of the paper with the image. Shade every part of the paper with a pencil having a dark graphite tip. Put the paper on the surface to be burnt and begin to trace out the image. The line of the image will be left on the surface.

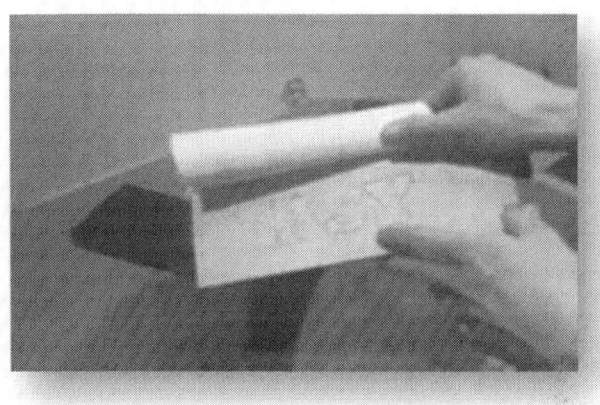

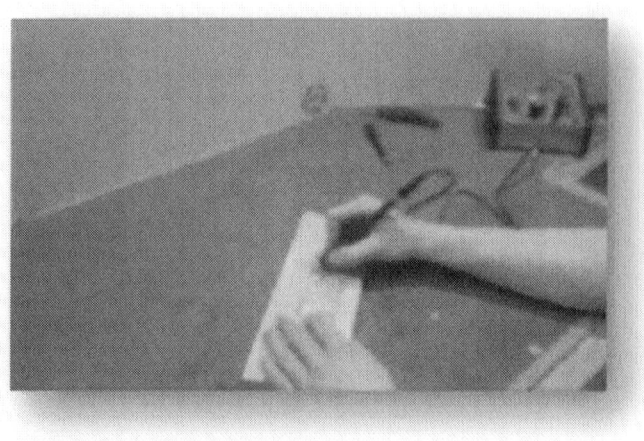

## *Cleaning of the Pen Tips*

To have perfect strokes devoid of unwanted burns, a clean tip should be used. With continuous usage and burning of materials with your pen, the tip will inevitably begin to accumulate carbon from the burning process and also resins from the sap of the wood. The tip will then appear black with a coat of dark, unsightly residue.

If the pen tip is used in this state, the burn lines on your work will be darker than you intend for it to be. The heat transfer to the pen tip will not be evenly distributed, and heat will also be easily lost, causing loss of time that will be spent reheating the pen.

In the cleaning processes of my pen, I employ two methods that have always worked for me; a red oxide cleaning compound and an emery cloth. In addition to these two methods, I clean my tips as often as I can immediately I notice that the carbon has started to build up.

To start the cleaning process of your tips at any point in time, switch off the burning unit and remove it from the power source, and keep it aside for a few minutes to cool off. The cleaning materials can be easily sourced for at the hardware stores around you.

In making use of the red oxide compound, I cover a leather strop with the oxide and then gently drag the tip over the strop for a few seconds or minutes until the original color of the tip is regained. You can then get a clean piece of cloth to wipe the tip to take care of any leftover dirt.

Arrange the emery cloth into a compact square shape to protect your fingers and place it over the tip and pull gently. Do not pull too hard as this might cause a bending of the burning wire at the tip of the pen.

## *Sealers*

After the pattern has been burnt into the work surface, it might be required that you apply some sealing finishers to the surface to prevent the project from distortions from environmental conditions and other artifacts that might lessen the artistic value of your work.

Not all burnt surfaces require sealing; e,g: paper and cotton. If you have burnt on leather, an oil-based sealer might be needed to prevent moisture from damaging the project.

With wood, however, sealing with oil, acrylic spray sealer or varnish is highly required. When you are through with burning the image, proceed to apply a series of coating on the work surface. The wood sealers are available in gloss sheens, semi-matte and matte. It does not have any effect on the tone of the wood surface. A 50 - 50 mixture of linseed oil and turpentine make your work shine and also ensure that you follow the instructions of the manufacturer when applying the coatings. Always ensure that you allow proper drying times between multiple coatings. As a safety precaution, properly make do away with any oil-coated rag once you are through with it. Get a bowl of water with some detergents and properly immerse and wash the cloth. If the oil-coated rag is left lying around your workspace, it might lead to a fire outbreak. A point to note is that when you apply oil coatings to your work, it will change the color of the wood into a dark tone, and this will also apply to your work.

When polyurethane coating is used on your project, the natural tone of the wood is maintained. This, however, is not the case with other wood varnish types that might give a coloring that you might not necessarily want and change the eventual outcome of your work.

## *The Wood Patina*

As a piece of wood grows old, its color gradually changes into a darker hue. For example, the white pine that has a white coloring when it is just cut and gradually becomes amber yellow after several years. Woods that are traditionally used for pyrography such as the basswood and birch do become dark brown with age. This change in coloring of the wood can make the pattern burnt into it appears to be disappearing. If the patterns burnt into the wood are light in color, there is a high probability that such patterns will disappear. As the wood changes color into a darker hue, the light-colored patterns are submerged and eventually disappear. This is a natural process that will always happen, and to preserve your artwork, you can take a few steps to reduce these potentials of your work losing out in the end to the aging of the wood.

Before starting with any wood burning project, carry out a proper survey on the type of color changes that will take place in the wood as it ages. For woods that will undergo considerable color change into a darker hue, your burning should be done in very dark shades and tones. Stay away from any light pale color burning on such wood types.

Make use of sealing agents that will restrict the effects of the ultraviolet radiation from the sun. The sealer considerably cuts down the process of oxidation, which can lead to the formation of patina in the wood. Vanishes and oil finishes that will bring about the darkening of the wood should be avoided. Birchwood, when varnished with Tung oil or Danish oil, will lead to the formation of darker brown hues as the wood ages. If you take your time to factor the risks associated with the type of sealers and woods to use on your pyrography works, you can be rest assured that your projects will stand the test of time.

## *Your Safety*

You must put in safety measures around your workspace before you begin wood burning. With wood burning, a considerable amount of heat is produced by the pyrography tool. The tip of the pen is always almost hot while the machine is switched on, and even when it does not appear red hot, it is still extremely hot and can cause severe burns. When handling the tip, it is best to have the mindset that this piece of equipment is always hot, even when it might not be. Be cautious always.

Have a piece of paper right next to you on the worktable to always gently place the pen against to check if it is hot. If the pen is hot, the paper will either darken or burn.

If you want to change the nibs of the pen, do ensure that it is cool before trying to removing it and fixing in another. While working, you might want to carry on without been interrupted by the break of having to change the nib; this is where patience and a sense of self-preservation should come in. Switch off the machine, go into the kitchen and make some coffee and allow some time for the nib to cool down before attempting to make the switch. This advice is not just for when you want to change the nib, but also for the burning pen itself too. If you have been working for a relatively long period, most times, the pen will start to get warm then hot. At this point, switch off the machine and take a well-deserved break.

When you are taking a break or carrying out some other duties, do not at any time drop your pen carelessly on the workbench without properly securing it, if it is on or not. The ideal thing to do if you are to put down your pen in the middle of burning is to switch it off and place it in a pen rest constructed of non-flammable materials.

Some pyrography machines are designed in such a way that you can place the pen on a stand attached to the machine when it is not in use. If your machine does not have this feature, switch it off and place your pen on a ceramic tie or some other non-flammable material.

When burning on wood, your workspace should be cross-ventilated. This allows for the fumes produced to be safely evacuated from the space as inhalation of the smoke for a long time can cause serious health hazards. To aid faster dispersion of the smoke, installation of a fan within the space to create a vacuum towards which the fumes produced are sucked towards would also help. The fan should not be pointed directly towards your work table as it will blow the fumes straight at you, and it will also cause the burning pen to cool down faster than you might want it to.

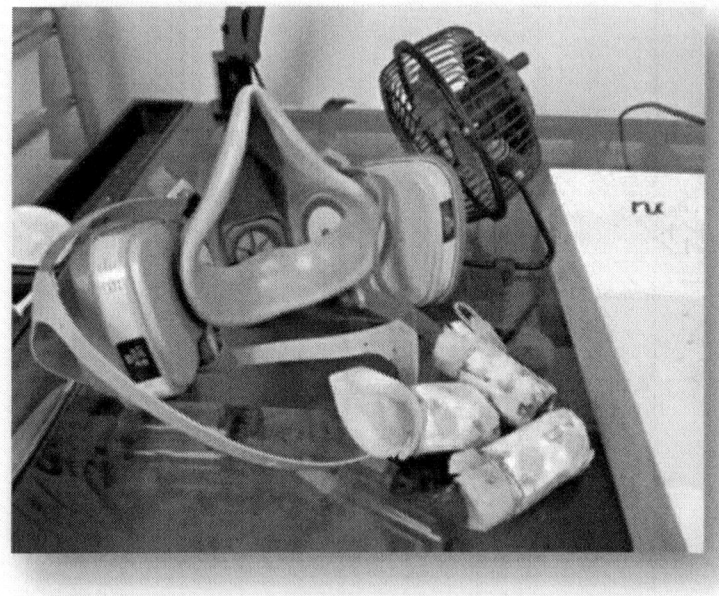

You should also have sufficient lighting within the workspace and even devoid of litter and scraps that can cause accidents. Clean the area regularly by removing items that may interfere with your work.

You should get some form of protection for your worktable to keep to the barest minimum burns that are likely to occur on it. You can get a protective mat or a piece of hardwood to be used as a protective material for your table.

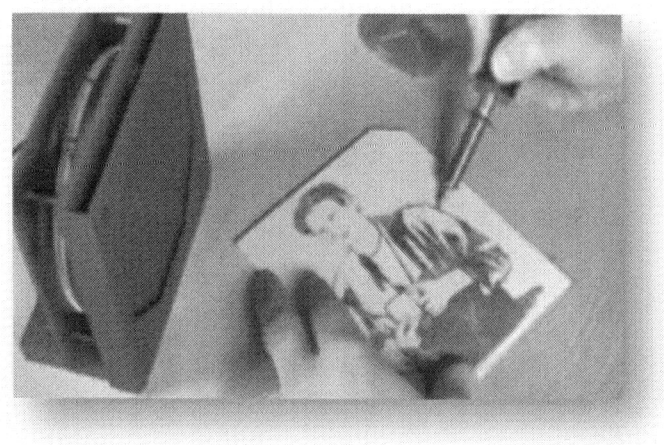

Your workspace should not at any time have any flammable materials, chemicals, or any other items that react quickly with heat close by. Your workspace should be childproof. The locks to the room should be in place at all times when you are working and when you are not within the space.

The connecting wires of the pen to the machine should be as free as possible. Make sure that it is not tangled up and doesn't come near the tip of the pen when you are burning or not. If the wires become tangled and you do not straighten it out, the quality of your work would be affected in addition to your machine and pen been potentially damaged. To untangle the wires of the burning machine, switch off the device, set down the pen, and give it some time to cool down properly before you proceed with untangling the wires.

Before you start burning, make sure that you are in a sitting position that is as comfortable as you can be. Sitting or standing in an awkward position will get you tired; your hands will hurt, and sores may likely develop.

So you are now burning some amazing patterns on your wood surface, do not get carried away with how the image is developing and burn your fingers. Your fingers should always be at a distance from the burning wood and also not too close to the pen element.

Sometimes we tend to overlook minor faults in our machines and continue to use it until it becomes a hazard. If you notice that your device is malfunctioning in any way, stop using it immediately. Some of the signs which are pointers to faulty equipment include and are not limited to humming sounds, sparks, etc. Immediately take your machine to a certified repairer for it to be fixed.

## CHAPTER TWO

## The Pyrography Machine and You

This section is dedicated to getting you familiar with your machine, though there might be parts that don't apply to your machine, you will surely get a thing or two that will be useful in how you deal with your new-found friend.

Source of Power

Read the manual that came along with your unit thoroughly on how to connect it to a source of power, making use of the cable that came together with it. The power cord should have uninterrupted access to the power source without it been hindered by equipment in your workspace. Sometimes your work table may be a bit far from where the power socket is located, in a case like this, an extension box will come in handy. The power cord should be straight and not coiled up or have an object placed on it.

## *Attaching the Burning Nibs*

It is most likely that your burning unit has a variety of nibs that came with the package. With these attachments that will make your project more pleasing to the eyes, you should take them on several practice runs to familiarize yourself with them before embarking on any significant projects. Switch off the unit from the power source while you try out your hand at fitting and unfitting the nibs from the pen. This will enable you to ascertain if a nib is securely fitted into the notch on the pen that it is meant to be in. The nib must be fixed appropriately into the pen for you to get a proper job devoid of errors produced.

## *Practice holding the burning pen*

Take hold of the pen and see which grip you are most comfortable with. Since you will be holding the pen for an extended period, you should hold the pen in a way that won't cause you sore muscles.

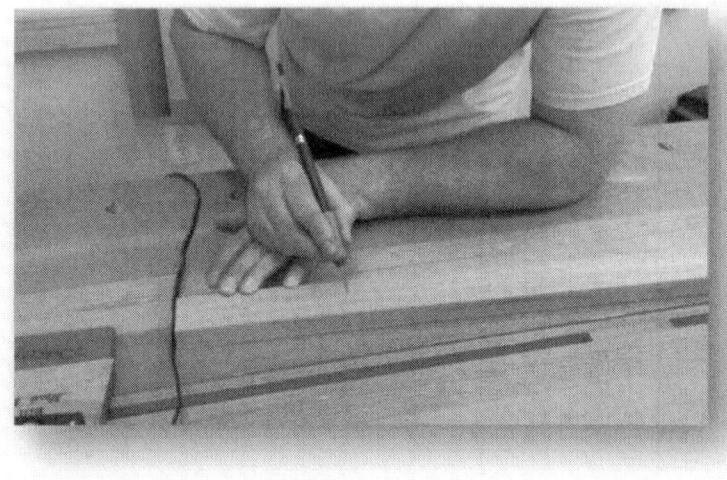

## *Powering on the Unit*

The pen should be in its holder before the unit is turned on. This is a safety precaution that you must practice at all times. Do not, at any point in time, leave the pen and the nib lying carelessly on the workbench or on your project as it can result in serious bodily harm or fire outbreaks. Some units come with a switch installed on it if you have this type, you will have to first switch on the power from the main source before turning on the switch on the unit itself. If your unit has no power button on it, however, that means that the only way you can power it on is directly from the main power source.

## Temperature Change

After powering on the unit, play around with the temperature settings on the unit and practice with burning on sample pieces of wood.

## Powering off

After you are done with practicing or a burning project, safely return the nib into its holder. Then proceed to switch off the unit from the power sources. You can also take time out to check how long it takes for the nib of the pen to cool down. You can do this by holding the nib against a piece of wood through an interval of a few minutes. Be aware at every point in time the location of the nib to avoid getting burnt.

# CHAPTER THREE

## The Pen Tips

Pen tips vary in how they are designed and the functions they carry out. Every type of pen is unique in the type of burn, width, and tone it will create when used for pyrography. For example, the ball tip and loop pens produce dark and pronounced lines while the curved shader or thin-edged spear tip will give you deep, thin lines.

As a starter, the set of tips that you should be making use of should be comprised of the following;

Flat spoon-shaped shader

A tight bent loop writing tip

Curved-edged spear shader

Ballpoint writing tip

Wide-wire square tip shader

Tips of these types will cover almost any kind of project you may want to carry out as a beginner. As you progress with this craft and become more confident in your craft, you can then source and begin to make use of professional tips.

Tips come in various sizes, names, and shapes. This variance is dependent on the manufacturer from which you got your equipment from.

Some pens have the tip permanently fixed, while others can be changed. In the pens with fixed tips, the wire for burning is joined together with the pen and cannot be removed at all. On the other hand, the pens that have tips that can be changed allows you to buy as many tips as you want to make use of with the pen.

Some brands of pens are built to uniquely function with the electrical makeup of that particular pyrography machine. You may, however, come across machines that allow the user to make use of pens from other brands on their machines. This is, however, not advisable as your unit may malfunction. In buying a new unit, take into consideration the ergonomics of the pen, the power rating, the connection between the unit and the pen, and other features that will offer you a seamless burning experience.

The ball tipped pens are available in varying diameters; the smaller diameter tipped pens are used for the construction of thin lines, and the pens with a larger diameter are for the formation of more extensive, thicker lines. The primary function of this type of pen is for the filling of solid work, scrubbing, and shading.

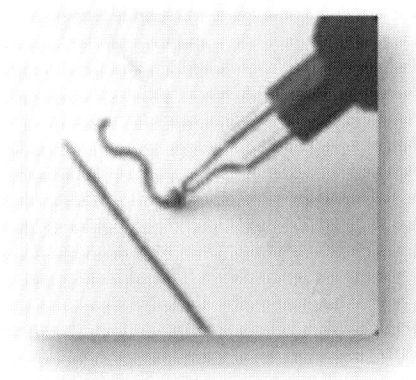

Ball point pen

## Writing and Outlining

The outlining pattern can be added to your work to make it more attractive. A cool temperature on the pen can be used to form the lines, and then you can proceed to burn your desired style lightly. After you are through with the shading, go over the lines again, but this time making use of higher temperature to a medium temperature setting. Don't just stick to one uniform line width; alter the thickness to make your work more appealing. The project that you are working on will determine if it is to be outlined or not. In projects already containing different tones, the inclusion of outlines may not be necessary. If you are burning the image of a natural setting, then there is almost no need for outlines, or you can add very minimal lines.

## Fill Texturing

To build a solid fill area, a high or medium temperature setting will be sufficient in addition to making use of a ball-tipped pen and lift and touch stokes of your hand. Closely filling the dots together will make the space appear in a darker tone. A medium temperature setting is more desirable than a higher temperature setting, as it can bring about the dot spilling and bleeding into areas you don't want it to get into.

## The Scrubbie Shading Technique

The ball tipped pen can be employed in creating short and small scrubbie strokes to bring about an equally distributed shading of your burns. To create a scubbie, carry out a well-regulated to and fro motion with your hands for relatively straight lines, or you can also create semi-circular, closely joined together lines. The lines should be tightly packed together in varying layers to give a dark tone to that particular space.

### Fine Lines Formation

The temperature setting for this burn is of no importance as all you need to do is set the tip of the pen in a straight position to the wood surface. With this, you can create straight even lines for outlines, the accent of shading. If you make use of low or medium temperature, the lines will appear in light tones, and with a higher temperature setting, the lines will come out dark.

### Texture Patterns

With the loop writing tip, you can create any type of texture pattern you desire. Hatched patterns, curls, curved lines, circles are perfect forms of textures that you can form with the loop writing tip. To make the tonal value appear light, your lines should not be too packed together, and if you want the area to appear darker, then the lines should be more tightly packed together.

## *The Flat Spear Shader*

This burning tip has a pointed or rounded tip with a flat surface. It also has a bent tip, and they are also referred to as spoon shaders, and for it to work efficiently, you need to set the temperature at highest due to the thick metal tip.

In scrubbie shading with this tip, the flat side of the pen should align directly with the wood while you draw fast short lines. The shader can be pulled up a little with the tip allowed to move quickly in creating curved shading motions.

## *The Curved-edge Spear Shader*

The spear shader has a bulkier tip than the curved-edge spear shader; thus, it can give thicker and dark lines without a higher temperature setting. You also get to create a light, thin burn without the formation of a dark point on the work surface, unlike when you make use of the ball tipped pen.

With the structure of the tip, the formation of long shading strokes can be formed. You place the tip against the surface and pull slowly as the shades are created.

## *The Wide-wire Square Shader*

This is the tip that both beginners and professionals should have in the toolkit. The structure of the tip makes it able to shade with thick stokes faster. If you are working on a large piece of art that requires plenty of shading and filling, this tip will help you get that done in a few minutes instead of spending the whole day on the task.

In some machines, you will find that the pen has parts that have been created to be fitted with nibs that are customized from Nichrome. To make the nibs secure into the holding parts, a screw can be used.

As you become more proficient in this art, you can look to building your specialty nib if you don't want to go with what the manufacturers have in store for you. The Nichrome wire can be bent into any shape you wish to as the project at hand demands. You can make the nib either tiny or thick to make light burns or thick and darker burns.

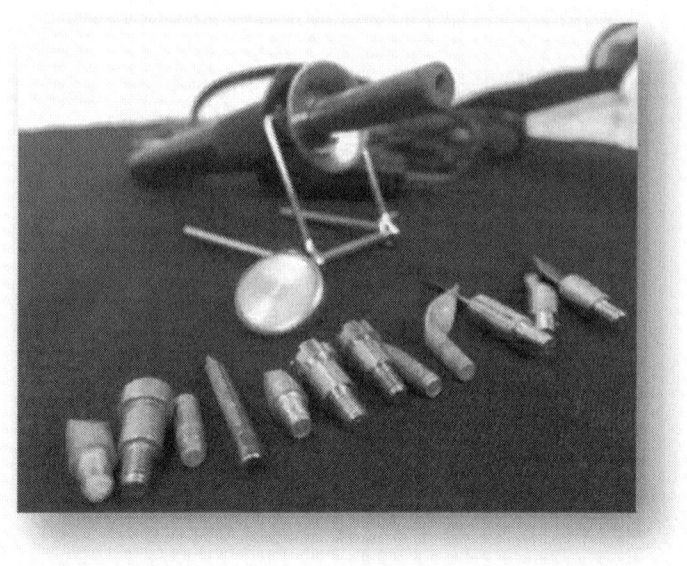

## *The Position of your Hand*

It doesn't matter the brand, type of the tip, or the pen been used for a burning project; the position of your hand holding the pen determines the curves of the lines been burnt, the pressure you apply to the burn, and how long the strokes get. Your burning pen should be held the same way you hold your writing pencil or pen. When the burning pen is held correctly, your hands won't get tired quickly, and the incidence of soreness and inaccurate burns won't occur.

To hold your burning pen the ideal way, your fingers should form a relaxed hold spread between the thumb and index finger at the tip at an angle of forty-five degrees to the surface of the burning wood. When you reduce the angle, a thick burn will result, and increasing the angle with the work surface will give you a thin burn line.

Do not form the habit of allowing your hands to lay on the work been burnt as this does not give you the freedom to move with ease, and it affects the length of the burn lines. To attain equilibrium between your hand holding the pen and the project, your pinky finger can rest on the surface of the work and gives the pen tip a firm grip to allow you control all aspects of the movement necessary for a stress-free burning.

## How to hold a Pyrography Pen

It goes without saying that with a pyrography project, you will be spending a lot of time holding your pen. With this at the back of your mind, you should aim to be at ease without any form of stress building up over the hours due to a lousy pen holding habit. To get started, you need to consider critically the type of pen you use when writing with a pencil and a pen. Are you comfortable with a pen with bulk or that which is relatively light without girth? When you have sorted out this first hurdle, you can then proceed with picking a machine that has a pen with characteristics suitable to your hands.

You hold the pyrography pen in the same fashion that you do with your drawing pencil or writing pen. However, a new variable is thrown into the mix, heat that is generated from the pen during the burning process.

Your fingers should be at a distance from the burning tip to reduce the sensation of heat that would most likely be generated but not too far to affect the holding of the pen and the work.

When shopping for a pyrography machine, look out for those whose pen has protective mechanisms like the finger guard or some form of insulation that reduces the amount of heat transferred to your fingers. The protective barriers give you a firmer hold on the pen.

Another tip is to get a first-hand feel of the pen before making a purchase. You can do this by practicing with a pen your friend has or from a hardware store. This will help shape your buying decision. You should be relaxed and be one with the machine you are going to buy. The machine itself should be a reliable piece of equipment that won't be giving you any forms of problem. The pen, which is an essential part of the unit, should fit into your hands and should feel like part of your fingers.

There should not be any form of second-guessing or doubting your compatibility with the pen as the eventual outcome of this relationship would be expressed in your projects. Take your time and explore all available options before buying a pyrography machine.

# CHAPTER FOUR

## Burning Lines

You have the passion, you took the first step and got a unit, now you have this book in hand, the next logical move is to burn curves, lines and other patterns on your choice of surface. You won't jump into a large project without any prior experience; no, you would need to practice over a period. How fast you can graduate into burning that all-important first project will be determined by how important you consider the next few steps.

## The First Burns

Get a nib and attach it to the pen, switch on the unit, and adjust the temperature between low to medium heat. Hold the pen comfortably and then move onto burning simple figures, letters, lines, dots, and any other thing that comes to your mind. Make sure that you are holding the pen correctly in such a way that it won't cause any discomfort or affect the outcome of your work. Adjust the temperature settings for different burns and look closely at how it turns out.

## *Lines*

After the last step, you can then try out your hand at burning relatively straight lines and curves. Fix the appropriate tip and form the different types of lines on the sample piece of wood. Carry out this process repeatedly. Your ultimate aim should be the ability to burn lines that are relatively consistent in fluidity, burn marks, and smoothness.

## *Direction Alteration*

This is the next stage once you have been able to perfect the art of burning lines. With you through with burning straight lines, how can you handle the inclusion of angles, alteration of the direction of flow? A change in direction and addition of angles to the straight burn lines will give a new dimension to your work, which has confined space for you to work.

## *Change of Speed*

With the previous steps taken care of, now is the time to change the speed and contact time of the nib with the surface of the wood. Burn marks that are made with a slow speed produce a thick burn that appears solid while quick burns are for features that add finesse to your project.

## Play around with different nibs

The steps listed out should be tried with a variety of nibs as available with your burning unit. The nibs all have unique advantages, and it is up to up to discover where the nibs in your unit will work best for you. This is a path that only you can walk as you set your imagination free.

## Shading Methods for Beginners

This is a start guide for shading on your projects by the joining of lines and curves to set up part of the project for darkening/shading. With constant practice, you will soon be able to churn out artworks with varying tones of shades.

## Shading Light Tones

Pick up a shading nib, preferably one with a broad tip, and adjust the temperature to low. Begin shading with fast, even consistent hand movements. The lesser the amount of times the nib goes over a particular area, the lighter the tone will be. To generate a light tone, do not allow the nib to spend too much time against the surface of the wood to prevent too much burn from occurring.

## *Shading Dark Tones*

Make use of the same broad shading nib you used in creating the light tones, adjust the temperature to either high or medium. Shade the area of interest a couple of times by going over and over until the tone of dark color you want is obtained. Keeping the nib against the wood for extended periods will also generate a darker tone.

## *Progressively Darker Tones*

Using a broad shading nib, adjust the temperature of your unit to a low heat setting. Start with shading an area of the project in a light tone and then start from one part of the work, shading it darker as you go from one end to the other. Go over this same process a few times, applying a little more pressure and shading than the previous shade until you are satisfied with the result. Your aim with this method of shading is to make one part of the image darker than the other in a simple graduated fashion.

Other than making use of the broad shading nib and the shading technique, you can also employ the use of the various nibs you have in the toolkit. A gradual change in tone can be brought about by gradually reducing the concentration of burn dots from one area to another. Experiment and see what turns up!

# CHAPTER FIVE

## Your Choice of Wood

Picking the right wood is an essential part of the whole process of creating a fantastic wood burning project. For your projects to turn out just the way you have in mind, go for woods that have a beautiful grain and light in color. This combination gives you the leeway to shade as smooth as you want and also produce amazing contrast. Examples of woods that you can use include; lime, sycamore, maple, holly, beech, etc.

Every piece of wood is unique in its own way. There will be markings, arrangement of grains, distortions, odd shapes, etc. that confers a character to that piece of wood you are using for your project. These natural formations that appear on the wood should not be seen as a disadvantage; instead, you should embrace it as part of the whole image you are trying to create. Look for ways in which you can integrate these aspects of the wood into your project. If the wood of interest is soft, it will burn fast, leading to a buildup of carbon and resin on the nib, and if you are working on a project with delicate and elegant details, it would be a problematic situation. If the wood is quite hard too, the drawing of lines may not be regular, and the nib of the pen will keep getting caught on the wood.

As stated earlier, avoid any form of processed woods or fiberboards.

## Burning Words in Wood

Pyrographing the surface of the wood is an artistic challenge that adds a unique feature to otherwise bland items. Burning wood can be used as a means of also marking your item, decorative, and for other purposes.

## *Getting the Wood Surface Ready*

To get started, you first have to select the wood of your choice; generally, light-colored and relatively softwoods are better to be used for wood burning. When selecting your wood, also look out for woods with a minimal amount of grain as it allows for more natural burning of straight lines without distortions.

The surface of the wood should be smooth, and sandpaper used to smoothen it out and remove any bumps and wood strands. If you burn on just any wood surface that has not been smoothened, you will still get your project at the end, but it won't come out as fine as it would have been if you had made use of a clean and smooth surface.

## *Transferring Letters to the Surface*

You can transfer the letters to the wood surface by making use of a template and carbon paper with a pencil. It can also be done by drawing directly to the wood surface through freehand drawing with a pencil. For beginners, however, I would advise that you make use of an already prepared template to guide you through this process before you graduate to freehand drawing.

The letters to be burnt to the wood surface can be downloaded from your computer, or you can draw it yourself first on a piece of clean paper. If the letters are gotten from your computer, print it out. After printing out the letters from your computer, first, place the carbon paper with the dark carbon side-lying directly on the surface of the wood before setting the paper with the letters on the carbon paper. Then proceed to carefully trace out the letters onto the wood surface with a pencil.

### *The Image Transfer Pyrography Tip*

There are ingenious ways of copying images or letters to the surface of the wood and at the same time, burning. This method involves using a photocopied image or letters by using the pyrography pen. The Image transfer pen is a specialty tip crafted for this purpose. To start with, photocopy the letters of images that you want to burn, place the paper with the image side down directly on the wood surface. The image transfer tip is then used to heat the paper, which results in the transferring of the image onto the wood. The heat from the image transfer tip breaks down the photocopier ink in the paper allowing it to be absorbed directly by the surface of the wood.

This method won't go through if you make use of a printed image; it would only work with photocopied images.

## *Your tools*

Buy a wood-burning unit that fits your personality and budget. The price of wood-burning units can be on the high side for professional setups or relatively cheap, depending on your spending powers. After you have gotten your unit, you will then have to pick a tip to use. The type of tip to be used will depend on the details you want to be burnt into a particular area of your work.

Some wood-burning unit manufacturers have tips that have unique and distinctive designs at the tips. These tips, which might have images, numbers, or letters, can be burnt directly to the wood surface by pressing the tip firmly against the wood surface. With such tips as these, you don't have to stress yourself over burning precise images and letters to the wood surface. The downside when using such tips is having to switch the tips now and then once you are done using it. Ensure you maintain every safety precaution when swapping out the tips. Switch off the unit and place the pen in its holder. Then make use of a pair of pliers to take out the tip and replace it with another.

When the tip is in place, switch on your unit and heat it to the desired temperature before burning to ensure that you get the right type of burn.

## Putting the Wood Burner to use

The wood burner should be held in a firm grip just like you would with your pen or pencil. This is to make sure that your hands are comfortable and that the burner doesn't drop from your hands. When burning, there is no need to press too hard on the surface of the wood as a burner when appropriately heated will do its job. Applying a little pressure will result in light burns, and to get dark burns, press your burner firmly against the surface to the wood.

## Constant Speed

At the start of your wood-burning experience, to keep your lines fairly regular, try as much as you can to keep your hand and the burner moving at a regular and constant speed over the surface of the wood. If the speed of the burner across the surface of the wood is not consistent, you would most likely get some lines darker than other parts of the wood. This is because the wood burner spent more time on that part of the wood compared to the other parts where your hand moved faster over. To perfect this making of consistent lines, you need to practice before carrying out any major project.

## *Burning the Numbers or Letters*

The burning of the letters should be done in one single consistent stroke if you can. Once you start with a line, do not stop at any point unless when you get to the end of the letter. Some letters can be finished with one single stroke, while others require two or three strokes, which can be a combination of curves and straight lines.

## *Temperature Alteration*

There may be a need for you to alter the temperature of the burner, depending on your choice during the burning process. If burning and you discover that the burns are too light, you will have to increase the temperature of the burner. The temperature of the burning is also dependent on the wood type and the method of pyrography that you are employing for the current project. This aspect is an indicator that your burning unit should have temperature control as it makes your job easier. If the unit is lacking a temperature control feature, you will find it hard controlling how dark or light your burn lines are. To effectively use such a unit, you will have to switch it off to cool a bit to get light-colored burn lines and switched on again to get darker lines.

## *Darkening the Letters*

Some of your projects may require you to fill in the letters with thick, dark lines. After the first burn, you will have to return to the letters and go over the lines with the exact pressure and fluidity you applied during the first round. When filling in the letters, the tip of the pen should be changed into a bigger one. This will make the filling faster with fewer chances of errors occurring.

The letters burnt into the surface of the wood will look just fine, but you should go a step further by adding some flourish and other little additions to make your project stand out. These little additions will not only add artistic value to your work, but it also serves as an avenue for you to derive some form of pleasure from the whole process. To make the application of the little additions easier, bring the specialty tips into play. Brand tips come in various shapes and sizes in an almost infinite number of designs that you can add to your project.

## *Final Applications*

This has been treated earlier in the book. With the varying types of treatments available for your finished work, it is only natural that you try out the varnish on a scrap of wood to have a look at how the finished product will turn out. This would prevent costly errors that can ruin all your hard work.

Since the wood ages and brings about a gradual fading of the burnt patterns, putting the work in direct sunlight will only hasten the process. Pyrography arts are best suited for indoors, and if you must place it outside, you should set it up under a shade. Also, a coat of spar vanish will protect the work against the elements. The ultraviolet radiation of the sun won't be able to penetrate the varnish applied.

To keep your project in the same pristine condition as at when you made it, you can apply several layers of varnish. After applying the first layer, wait for it to dry properly before applying another coat. Also, to be taken into consideration is the coating of the work every three to four years.

Varnishes and oils have directions on how to be used and stored. Ensure that you read the manual that comes with such products and follow it to the letter.

If your project will be taking on some form of painting, carry out a sample painting on a piece of wood, then apply the varnish or oil to check if they will react. In all, have an open mind and be ready to put new ideas to work.

# CHAPTER SIX

## Exercises

## Wood Burning Project Ideas

We are finally here. In this section, I will be guiding you through a few basic projects that will sharpen your skill and build your confidence in the art of pyrography. The materials, supplies, and any other equipment needed for the woodwork can be readily sourced from the hardware store, or you can just as well go online and order for what you need.

### Key Holders

These are unique items that you can burn on as a beginner or a professional. The key holders come in wooden square shapes, or they are available in other forms in your local hardware store. Some come with holes already drilled, or you can carry drill the holes yourself.

## Supplies

Blank wooden key holders

Pencil

Pyrography unit

Erase

Bladed nib

Spear nib

Craft knife

Spoon point nib

Key holder rings

## Directions

- Use your pencil to draw the image or writing on one side of the key holder, or you can get pictures or letterings from your PC that you can transfer to the key holder.

- Make use of a carbon paper or a photocopied image in transferring the image onto the key holder through the aid of a pencil or an image transfer nib. This method of transferring using a paper is the easiest and fastest way as it is repetitive, and you can transfer onto lots of key holders within a short period.
- Burn the lettering on the key holder employing the spear point nib at medium heat.
- If you have copied an image on the other side of the key holder, at medium temperature with a bladed nib burn the image with quick and delicately placed lines.
- Do not unnecessarily let your hand become too tired while trying to accommodate the key holder. Turn the key holder around to make it easier for you to burn.
- Using a spoon nib, shade the image, and letterings on the item. You can introduce an

element of gradient shading or whatever other forms of shading you want.

- Replace the nib with a spear point nib set to a high temperature. Then proceed to burn a fancy pattern around the edge of the key holder. Choose beautiful designs that will appeal to those you are going to give it to or sell to.

# Door Decorations

Our doors are most times bland without any information or patterns that make it a work of art. Your door should serve as a portal of communication and canvas at the same time. The designs you will be producing will be serving as eye candy and at the same time, acting as a source of information. So it's bye to the age of blank doors.

**Supplies**

Tracing paper

Craft knife

Bladed nib

Spoon point nib

Spear nib

Scissors

Pencil

Eraser

Pyrography unit

Adhesives

Masking tape

**Directions**

- Get blank wooden designs of various shapes and sizes.
- Using freehand drawing or an image copied from the internet, transfer it to the blank wood with your pencil. The image or lettering been copied should be something that is unique and makes you stand out.
- At medium heat setting, make use of a bladed nib to burn the outline of the images onto the wood. Be careful and deliberate as you burn the image. Ensure that the lines and curves are neat without any blemish.
- Shade with a spoon point nib at high-temperature setting. The shading gives the

design a more solid 3D effect. The dark areas of the image are shaded with the spoon nib, while you should make use of the spear nib in areas that are lighter in color. Apply stripped shades to the light areas.

- Apply a suitable adhesive type to the back of the project and the door and hang it.
- You can also drill a small hole on the artwork and hang it on your door.

## *Fancy Napkin Holders*

These well-designed holders are used during celebrations and dinners to add life to the dinner table. It is used to give off a sense of personalization to persons at the gathering as you can add details particular to each individual to the ring holder, which they can take away as souvenirs after the party. The ring holders can also be used as cardholders for your guests to identify their tables.

## Supplies

Blank napkin holders (ring or square shaped)

Tracing paper

Craft knife

Pyrography unit

Masking tape

Pencil and eraser

Shading nib

Spoon point nib

Spear nib

## Directions

- Pick up the tracing papers and cut them into sizes that will sufficiently cover the length and breadth of the napkin holders.

- Making use of images or letters you got from your computer or using freehand drawing, transfer the designs onto the napkin holders.
- Hold the tracing paper in place with the masking tape and use your pencil to transfer the lettering and patterns.
- At medium temperature with a spear nib, burn the copied images or letterings on the napkin holder. Be aware of the position of the nib relative to your fingers at every point in time.
- With the images and letterings burnt to the surface, it is time to add some attractive finishing. Fix the shading nib with a distinct pattern into the pen at high temperature and then using some force, press it into the surface of the wood and preselected areas.

## *Cup Coasters*

These items are the perfect starting projects for beginners like you. The relatively small sizes of the coaster surfaces make them a friendly attraction to burn on. You can burn the same design and pattern on several coasters, or you can as well integrate several varying designs on a set of cup coasters.

With wood-burning, you can add some personal touches to the coasters by making them unique and easily identifiable to a particular individual.

**Supplies**

Blank wooden cup coasters

Circle stencil

Pencil

Eraser

Pyrography unit

Ruler

Craft knife

Masking tape

Spoon point nib

Spear nib

Tracing paper

**Directions**

- Start with setting up a border using the pencil and ruler at about 12mm from the edge of the blank coaster. This creates an aesthetically pleasing addition to the coaster, and you might not need to burn it.
- Transfer your desired images into the area within the borders.
- The cup coasters can have individual personalities by the addition of varying designs burnt into them.
- Using a spoon point nib set to medium heat, shade the images, and design to be as clean as you can.

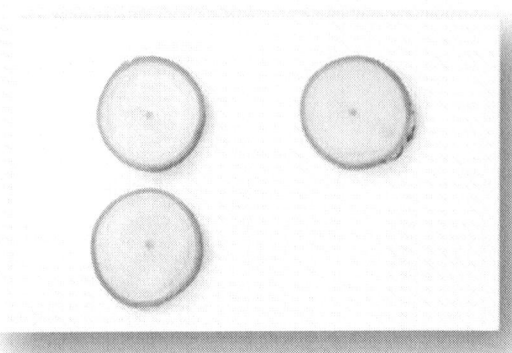

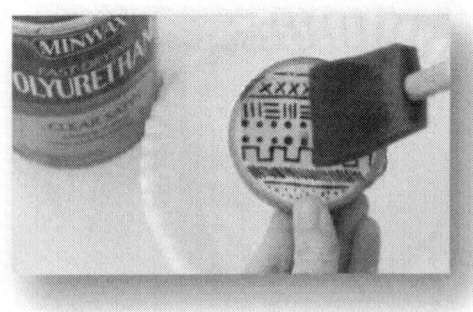

## *Picture Frame*

Frames are one ubiquitous item that you will find in almost any room you enter. It might be hung on a wall or sit on the table. Frames hold pictures that show happy times and serve as a portal for memories. Frames can either be circular, square, or rectangular, depending on your choice. It goes without saying that when shopping for your supplies and the frame, in particular, it should be devoid of any form of treatment.

**Supplies**

Picture frame (blank and untreated)

Masking tape

Pyrography unit

Tracing paper

Craft knife

Pencil

Eraser

Shading nib

Bladed nib

Spoon point nib

**Directions**

- Set up a border with a pencil and ruler at about 5mm from the outer and inner edges of the picture frame. The borderlines are temporary features that act as a guide on the areas where the burns are going to be carried out. So ensure that the lines are as faint as possible, but you should be able to discern where it is because you will be cleaning it after the burning is done.
- Set the temperature of the bladed nib to medium heat and burn the inner lines. Be neat and precise during this stage.
- Design the areas just on the inner border using a spoon point nib at high or medium

temperature. The pattern design should progress from the inner line out towards the edge of the picture frame.
- Place the patterns or designs you got from your computer onto the edges of the frame and trace making use of your pencil. You can also make use of freehand if you so wish.
- Adjust the temperature of the bladed nib to high or medium heat and burn the images that were transferred to the borderlines.

## *Hair Rings*

Nothing beats designing your jewelry collection. It signals your individuality and tastes. With your wood burned hair rings and bangles, you can change the way you look for any function. The challenge is getting blank rings or bangles; however, if you search enough, you will surely come across a supplier that will meet your specifications. You can burn words or lyrics that have a personal meaning to you on the wooden rings.

## Supplies

Wooden rings or bangles

Pyrography unit

Tracing paper

Pencil

Eraser

Shading nib

Spoon point nib

Spear nib

Masking tape

Craft knife

## Directions

- Get your tracing paper that fits the length and breadth of the wooden ring. Get your favorite quote or image and trace it onto the surface of the wood.
- Making use of the masking tape, fix the tracing paper properly to the surface of the wooden ring. Place the paper with the image or lettering that you want to transfer onto the tracing paper and transfer with your pencil.
- Adjust the temperature to high on the spear nib and burn the images or lettering that were transferred to the surface of the wood. Burn the outline of the letters while still leaving the inner parts unburnt for the moment.
- Fix in the spoon nib and set the temperature to high and continue the burning of the borders of the image or letters. Burn with free lines.

- Bring in an element of solidity by using a spoon point nib set to a high temperature. Shade areas by including dot gradients from one end to another.

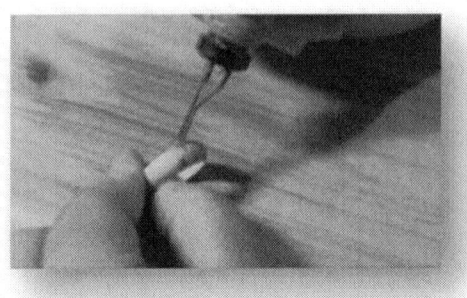

# Pyro Wall Clock

Having an artistically wood burnt wall clock in your room is a beautiful deviation from the norm. You don't have to go shopping to get one; this is one piece of art that you can create to stand out in any room in which it is placed. Let your blossoming skills come to life in building this art piece. Getting the required supplies for this project won't be hard as you can readily get it from your local hardware stores.

## Supplies

A wooden clock unit (the clock mechanism, the clock hands, and the clock hands)

12 fancy upholstery pins

Pyrography unit

Craft knife

Masking tape

Ruler

Spoon point nib

Spear nib

Bladed nib

Ink color of your choice

Protractor

Hand drill

Brush

Pencil

Eraser

**Directions**

- Make use of the protractor and ruler in equally marking out the face of the clock into a dozen parts.
- The total angle of the face of the clock is 360°, so each part of the dozen will be 30°.

- Get ready the border pattern that will fit in perfectly into the size of the clock you will be using. Copy the image or design pattern of your choice onto the tracing paper. Place the tracing paper on the wooden surface of the clock and use your pencil to transfer it. The pattern you will be moving should fit into each section, or it can be used for the whole surface of the clock in one transfer. Whatever method you decide to use is up to you.
- Set your bladed nib to either a high or medium temperature and burn the outline of the clock. The lines should be fluid and uniform, devoid of squiggly lines.
- With the borderline done, move onto the inner design of the clock. The design of the clock face should factor in the opening in the center from which the clock mechanism will be fitted.

- Gently set the tracing paper with the design onto the central part of the clock. Ensure you don't let the paper go out of position when you are transferring the image with your pencil. A masking tape will help you secure the paper in place during this process.
- Burn the central image with the bladed nib at high temperature. A clean and continuous line should be maintained at all times.
- After you are through with the burning, move onto shading areas where you want to show some form of solidness with a spear nib at medium to the high-temperature setting.
- A spoon nib should then be used to continue the shading by working on the outlines previous worked on with as much care as you can.
- Fill the design of the border with the spoon nib by forming a well-packed together

textured design. Hold the bowl of the spoon nib firmly against the clock surface, forming the textured marks in close proximity.
- Add other designs and patterns as you deem fit into the central and outer parts of the clock surface.
- Using your paintbrush, paint in the color of your choice into the image, numbering, and letters.
- Drill in holes into the divided sectors of the clock at about 1mm in diameter. This will serve as the location for the numbers. The clock should be held firmly in place when the drilling is ongoing.
- Insert the fancy upholstery pins into the drilled holes with care.
- Unpack the clock mechanism and fit it into the back of the clock before arranging the hands at the front.

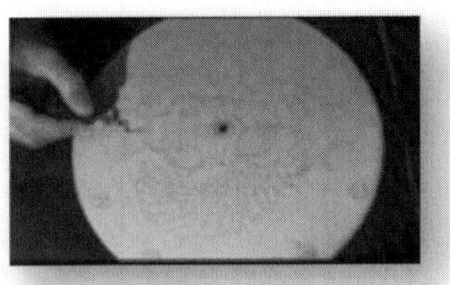

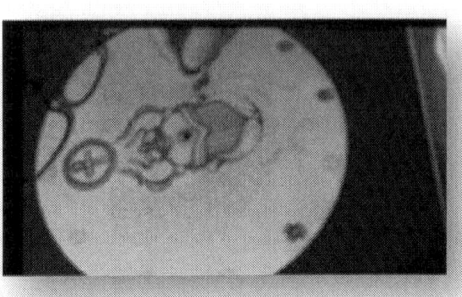

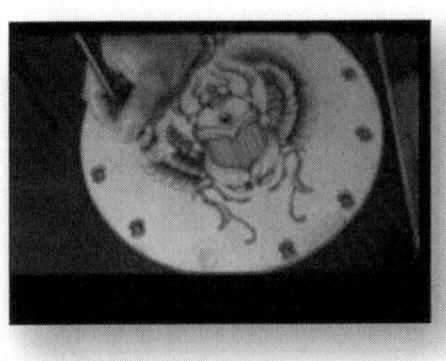

# Other Book(s) by the Author

***The Simple Beginners Guide to Cricut Explore Air 2: A Manual on how to Setup Cricut, Design Space, Cricut Project Ideas, Troubleshooting, and Essential Tips***

Are you interested in upping your craft game with the Cricut Explore Air 2 or any of the Cricut brands? You are here, and that is all that matters now. This is the guide that you need in this ever-morphing environment of designs. There is always something new to be learned in the world of Cricut if you are a professional or a newbie. Why hold onto yesterday's ideas that will make your work look outdated? It is time that you take a dive into the amazing world of the Cricut Explore Air 2 and other Cricut brands to learn and relearn some of the following;

- An introduction on what the Cricut machine is

- The different types of Cricut machines
- How to unbox and setup the Cricut Explore Air 2
- Understanding the different types of materials that you can work on with your Cricut machine
- Choosing the material settings
- How to use image files
- Installing and Uninstalling the Cricut Design Space
- Making use of Design Space
- Installing fonts from Design Space
- Uploading your image to Design Space
- The Basic set of the Cricut Tools kit
- Pairing the Cricut Explore machine through Bluetooth to the Computer
- Resetting the Cricut Explore Air 2 Machine
- Using Print and Cut in Cricut Design Space
- Vinyl tricks
- Amazing DIY Project Ideas
- Sample Projects

- Tips that a lot of folks overlook about the Cricut machine
- Maintenance for your Cricut machine
- Troubleshooting
  And so much more!

https://www.amazon.com/dp/1702647226

**A Guide to Wood Finishing for Beginners: A Step-by-Step Manual on How to Finish, Refinish, Restore, Stain, Dye and Care for your Furniture**

*This is the ultimate wood finishing guide for an exquisite project.*

Applying a well-thought-out and researched finish can bring out the beauty and shine in an otherwise bland work. On the flip side, a well-built and alluring piece of woodwork can be turned into an ugly duckling with a lousy finish.

Clayton M. Rines takes you on a journey through one of the aspects of woodworking that many crafters will rather avoid. He removes the cloud of mystery surrounding wood finishing. You will navigate the minefield of finish application, refinishing, and staining with ease like a pro. You will discover new and existing methods that work on how to select the best type of finish for your project, correct errors, prepare the wooden surface, and troubleshoot.

As a beginner or a pro, it is pertinent that you understand the basics of staining, coloring, and dyeing your wood. This will give you a wide array of options to play within any project, thus breaking down restrictions that might have been in place. When you fully understand the foundation of wood finishing, you will be able to bring out the hidden beauty of your wood, promote its longevity, and make the whole wood-crafting process a seamless experience.

*"A Guide to Wood Finishing for Beginners"* is packed with invaluable tips and hints that will enlighten you on the reasons why you should go through the process of finely finishing your wood, the methods to embrace, and what to avoid.

**You will learn the following and much more** ;

- Simple and safe method of applying spray finish
- The different types of solvents, oils, and varnish
- The types of wood and how to apply finish to them
- Stripping and Refinishing
- Stain and dye application
- Restoring furniture
- Water-based and oil-based finishes
- An easy to understand approach to the subject theme
- The beginners guide on polishing, spraying, sanding, etc

- Fixing mistakes

- Troubleshooting

Written with you in mind to help solve your wood finishing fears as a beginner or an experienced hand needing a bit of refresher, this is a must-get book.

**CLICK on the BUY button** to begin finishing your wood with style today.

https://www.amazon.com/dp/B08LPJ6C9Z

***The Simple Woodcarving Book for Beginners: Simple Techniques for Relief Carving, Easy Step-by-Step Beginner-Friendly Projects, and Patterns with Photographs***

Getting started with woodcarving or any other form of art can be a bit daunting. You are at a loss on the type of equipment and tools to purchase the simple projects that your skill level can start with. Mr. Clayon M. Rines has got you all covered with everything to get you started as a novice woodcarver or an experienced hand looking to refresh your wealth of knowledge.

The Simple Woodcarving Book for Beginners, Simple Techniques for Relief Carving, Easy Step-by-Step Beginner-Friendly Projects and Patterns with photographs is a personal guide with a passionate teacher. You will learn how to make those clean cuts in different ways, sharpening your tools and putting the finishing touches on your work.

Your desire to master this age-long art of woodcarving has brought you this far, and this passion will be fueled and guided with everything you will be learning from the pages of this book. Clayton M. Rines will expose you to secrets of the trade, such as the basic cuts, smoothening techniques, how to carve contours, and the essentials or relief carving.

The directions to follow for each method are clearly explained and accompanied by photographs to further breakdown the process. What do you need to get that first project done? This book in your hands, a few well-honed essential cutting tools and a piece of softwood, and you will be on your way to carving the most amazing and exquisite objects that will continuously recharge your bank account, serve as gift items to friends and loved ones and give you joy unlimited. With your desire to fully understand everything about carving in relief and producing masterpieces, this all-encompassing book on woodcarving will enlighten you and show you the best way to go about it.

From when the idea comes to you, the initial cut to the final finishing touches, these steps will guide you every step of the way; •Step-by-Step practice projects with visual guides to build your confidence levels• Types of woods, tools and your workspace, finishing •Basic and well-explained carving techniques• Detailed directions• Carving relief projects• Maintaining and keeping your tools well-honed and in perfect condition. It doesn't matter if you are a novice or a professional carver; this is the book you should get and expand your woodcarving horizon!

https://www.amazon.com/dp/B084P6T7Q3

*The Pyrography, Woodcarving and Leather Crafting Beginners Guide with Exercises: A Beginner Friendly 3 in 1 Manual with Instructions on Wood Burning, Leatherworking and Woodworking*

**The essential craft book for all time!**

This is the ultimate pastime book for folks of all ages and genders, which will keep you busy at any time of the day. This book is a compilation of three of my books on crafting covering;

- **Pyrography (Wood Burning)**

- **Woodcarving**

- **Leather Crafting**

The crafts thoroughly explained in this book will go a long way in honing your crafting skills and take you away from that everyday routine while you spend quality time in your workshop.

"The Pyrography, Woodcarving and Leather Crafting Beginners Guide with Exercises" is packed full of invaluable lessons, hints and guides that will bring out the craftsman in you.

As well as helping you develop crafting skills, you will also learn the importance of patience, building a focused and mindful attitude that is devoid of disturbances that are all around us.

Are you a bit confused about how to go about starting your first project? With your tools on your workbench and this book in front of you, and your journey towards crafting that masterpiece will be the most fun trip you have ever embarked on.

With your aim to have a grasp on what pyrography, leather crafting and woodworking are all about, this book covers everything that you need to know and much more.

Within the pages of this amazing book, you will learn;

Simple practice projects with illustrations to develop your confidence levels

How to shade, write and apply outlines

Variety of woods, equipments, finishing and your work bench

Simply and thoroughly explained wood carving methods

Temperature settings in wood burning

Importance facts about leather

Knowing what type of burning nibs to use

Cutting and making patterns

Stamping

Stitching

Embossing

Gluing

Coloring

Finishing

Beveling

How to source and care for leather

Projects

And so much more!

No matter the skill, project, or ideas you want to implement on your wood or leather piece, you will find all that in this book and much more!

**What are you waiting for? GRAB a COPY now!**

https://www.amazon.com/dp/B08HTG62H7

## *Leather Crafting Beginner's Manual: A Step-by-Step Illustrated Guide with Basic Leatherworking Projects and Techniques*

*Explore the fantastic world of leather crafting that will give you joy for ages!*

• Need to have manual for both beginners and experienced hands working with leather

• Detailed and well-explained facts about leather, tools, techniques, and projects to help you with leather crafting

• Become acquainted with the necessary methods through well-taught guides on the use of essential tools, leather preparation, and finishing.

• Understand and put to practice skills such as stitching, forming, braiding, molding, lacing and embossing

- Sequential photographic illustration of the different processes and tools

- Incredibly easy to craft projects for you!

Leather crafting is a timeless art that is not limited to any age bracket or skill level. If you are a pro in search of a brush-up material or a beginner needing proper grounding, Leather Crafting for Beginner's is your go-to manual for a fun crafting experience.

Clayton M. Rines introduce you to the foundations of leather, its structure, types, preparation, how to use embossing tools, awls, cutters, stamps, etc. He gives essential hints on how to braid, stitch and craft primary, intermediary, and difficult leatherworks.

## **This book contains;**

- Historical facts about leather

- Cutting and making patterns

- Stitching

- Stamping

- Gluing

- Embossing

- Beveling

- Coloring

- Finishing

- How to care and source for leather

- Projects

- And so much more!

No matter the skill, project, or ideas that you want to implement on your leather piece such as the making of a leather bracelet, cufflinks, pouches, passport cover, Leather Mason Jar Koozie, amazing scrap leather projects, etc., you will find all that in this book and much more!

**Begin your leatherworking journey today with that can-do attitude.**

**CLICK the buy button now!**

https://www.amazon.com/dp/B08KH3T1PS

## About the Author

Clayton M. Rines is a techie who lives in and around gadgets. Knowing what makes devices all around us tick is his life ambition, and he is always on the lookout for new ideas to everyday technological problems. Bringing solutions to your gadget issues, giving opinions and tips on how to get the best out of your devices, and bringing to you excellent news gives him so much pleasure. He is a DIY expert, naturalist and animal lover.

Clayton is from Sacramento, California and enjoys globetrotting, savoring new experiences, enjoying new cultures.

Printed in Great Britain
by Amazon